Foundations in RE>

Judaism

essential edition

Foundations in RE

Judaism

Ina Taylor

essential edition

Stanley Thornes Publishers (Ltd)

First published in 2000 by:
Stanley Thornes (Publishers) Ltd
Ellenborough House
Wellington Street
CHELTENHAM GL50 1YW
England

00 01 02 03 04 / 10 9 8 7 6 5 4 3 2 1

A catalogue record for this book is available from the British Library.

ISBN 0-7487-5194-7

Printed and bound in China by Dah Hua Printing Press Co. Ltd

Page layout by Ann Samuel
Illustrated by Steve Ballinger, Rosalind Hudson and Angela Lumley

Acknowledgements

With special thanks to Jeremy Michelson, Don Rainger and the Manchester Jewish Museum.

With thanks to the following for permission to reproduce photographs and other copyright material in this book:
Ahava: 84 (right); Steve Allen Photography: 6, 45; The Ancient Art & Architecture Collection: 13; ASAP: Lev Borodulin 25, 40, Kenneth Fischer 52, Richard Nowitz 55; Associated Press: 8 (right), 22, 29; CIRCA: 14, 16, 34, Barry Searle 65, 73; Sonia Halliday: 19, 32, 75; Robert Harding: 71; Nickolai Ignatiev/Network: 28; Image Select: Chris Fairclough 70 (top); The Jacob's Bakery Limited: 36, The Jewish Museum: 26, 31; Jewish National Fund: 80; Alex Keene/The Walking Camera: 41, 49, 54, 59; News International: 67, 85; Penguin Books: 30; Popperfoto/Reuters: 43; Rakusens Limited: 63; Paul Rogers/Times Newspapers Limited: 46; The Ronald Grant Archive: 20, 78; Springboard Education Trust: 47 (left); Martin Sookias: 12, 15, 35, 39, 50 (left), 53, 59, 62, 66, 68; Ina Taylor: 7, 24, 48, 57, 58, 61, 84 (left); Jerry Wooldridge: 47 (right), 70 (bottom right).

Quotes taken from an interview with Felicity Kendal reproduced with permission of Curtis Brown Ltd, London, on behalf of Danny Danziger. Copyright © Danny Danziger, 1999, 2000, p76; Institute for Historical Review for quote on p78; Ben Hammersley, Times Newspapers Limited, 2 September 1999 for the article on p85; Quotes taken from an interview with Esther Rantzen reproduced by kind permission of Weekend Magazine, p77.

Every effort has been made to contact copyright holders. The publishers apologise to anyone whose rights have been inadvertently overlooked, and will be happy to rectify any errors or omissions.

Note: Throughout the series BCE (Before Common or Christian Era) and CE (Common or Christian Era) have been used in place of the traditional BC and AD. The new terms are more acceptable to followers of non-Christian religions.

Contents

1.1 Symbols of Judaism

The menorah

There are many symbols of Judaism. In the middle of this window is the oldest one. It is a candlestick with seven branches. This is called a **menorah**. It reminds Jews of the oil lamp that used to burn in their temple. Some people say the menorah reminds them of the seven days of creation. Others say it is like the Tree of Life. Many Jews have a small menorah at home. The centre candle is called the servant. It is used to light the other six candles.

At the top of this window is **Hebrew** writing. You read it from right to left. This word is the name of God. The Hebrew writing is hidden in this picture as it is wrong to write God's name on paper which can be torn easily. Hebrew is also written on each candle in the menorah.

Palm leaves are a symbol of Israel. Grapes can be seen. This is because **wine** is used in many Jewish ceremonies. It means happiness. Pictures of lions and olives can also be used as symbols of Judaism but they are not here.

Star of David

The Star of David is a modern symbol for Judaism. The star has six points. It is named after King **David** who was a great leader. He reminds Jews today of hope and freedom. This picture shows the oldest carving of a Star of David in Israel. It dates from the second century CE.

Star of David.

Do you remember?

1 A _____ is the name of a seven-branched candlestick.

2 The writing in Judaism is in _____.

3 Grapes are shown because _____ is a sign of happiness.

4 King _____ was an important Jewish leader.

Do you know?

What does the menorah remind Jews of?

1.2 Beliefs about God

Jews believe there is only **one** God. God has always been there and does not die. They say there are no words to describe God. There is nothing else like God.

Their belief is summed up in the Shema. This is the most important Jewish prayer.

> **Hear O Israel, the Lord our God is one God, the Lord is one.**

One of the psalms says 'How clearly the sky reveals God's glory'.

Jews believe God created everything, even microscopic life.

God the creator

In Genesis it says God made everything out of **nothing**. Jews do not think creation happened once a long time ago. They think it goes on every day. Plants and animals are always growing. The weather and the seasons change. Jews say if you look at the wonders of creation, you can get an idea of how great God is. They also say the earth was made by God and people must not destroy it.

God and humans

Jews think God is greater than everything. He has a special care for his creation. God **loves** the people he made. He listens to their **prayers**. He is always ready to help them and has helped them in the past. Jews do not think people are like puppets. God does not pull the strings. People have free will. They can do what they like. Even if they ignore God, Jews think God still cares about them.

Even though God is great, Jews can talk to him. Because they want to show respect, many Jews do not use the word God. They say 'Almighty' or 'Him'. They may write G–d as well.

Can you remember?

1 Jews believe in _____ God.

2 They think he created everything out of _____.

3 God _____ the people he created.

4 People can speak to God through _____.

Do you know?

Why do some Jews write G–d and not the full word God?

1.3 The Covenant

It's a deal!

You make a deal when you buy something. If you want to buy a car, you fix the price with the seller. You agree to give them your money. They agree to give you the car. As a sign of this deal, you usually shake hands.

Jews believe God made a **deal** with them. It is called the Covenant.

The sign

God told the Jews to make a **sign** to show they agreed. They were told to circumcise all the males. This is a simple operation. The foreskin on the penis is cut off when a baby boy is born. You can see this being done on page 52.

It says in the Bible that God first told Abraham about the Covenant. Abraham was 99 years old. But he still did as God wanted.

God promised:
• to look after the Jews.
• to make them his **chosen** people.
• to give them a land of their own.

The Jews promised:
• to love God.
• to **obey** his rules.

Despite his age he circumcised himself! Then he operated on all the men in his tribe.

Some time later God spoke to Isaac, who was Abraham's son. God renewed the deal with Isaac. Later God renewed the Covenant with Jacob, Abraham's grandson.

Do Jews think they are better?

No. They think God made everybody equal. But they think being chosen means they have got special duties. They were the ones who agreed to keep God's rules. That isn't an easy thing to do.

A Promised Land

Jews believe God gave them the country called Israel. This country used to be called Canaan. It was also called Palestine. God said to Abraham, Isaac and Jacob, 'The whole land of Canaan will belong to your descendants for ever'.

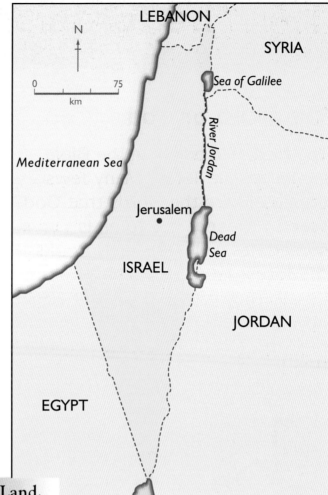

The Promised Land.

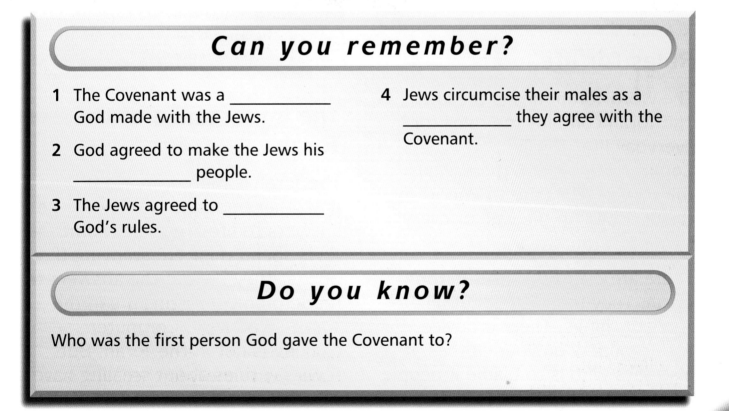

Can you remember?

1 The Covenant was a _____ God made with the Jews.

2 God agreed to make the Jews his _____ people.

3 The Jews agreed to _____ God's rules.

4 Jews circumcise their males as a _____ they agree with the Covenant.

Do you know?

Who was the first person God gave the Covenant to?

The word of God

The **first** five books in the Bible are called the Torah. Many Jews think they are the words that God gave to **Moses**. The Torah is sometimes called the Five Books of Moses. Jews study the Torah in detail. They want to find out about how God told them to live. Jews read the Torah in Hebrew because that was the language it was first written in.

Study is more important than prayer.

Rules for life

The word Torah means the law. The Torah contains the rules for everyday life. The Ten Commandments are there. Jews think these rules are so important they are put on the wall of every synagogue.

There are over 600 **rules** in the Torah. They tell Jews about all sorts of things. There is advice about mildew on your clothes. It also says who is to blame if people get hurt in a fight.

The Torah scrolls are kept safely in the ark. Above the ark are the Ten Commandments.

The importance of the Torah

The Torah is more important than any other book. Jews think all the answers to life are there. Some Jews spend their life studying the books. They believe the answers to modern day problems are in the Torah if you look. Computer hacking is not in the Torah. But Jews say rules about stealing have not changed.

Chinese Whispers?

The Torah was passed on by word of mouth first. Then it was written down. Some people say there is a danger that the words got muddled like they do in Chinese Whispers. But words can be carefully passed on. Nursery rhymes are handed on by word of mouth. The version of 'Humpty Dumpty' you know is the same as it was a hundred years ago.

Dead Sea scrolls

In 1947 hundreds of scrolls were found in caves by the Dead Sea in Israel. They are some of the oldest **writings** of the Bible. Jews were pleased to find that the words on them were the same as the ones on scrolls today.

A fragment of one of the Dead Sea scrolls.

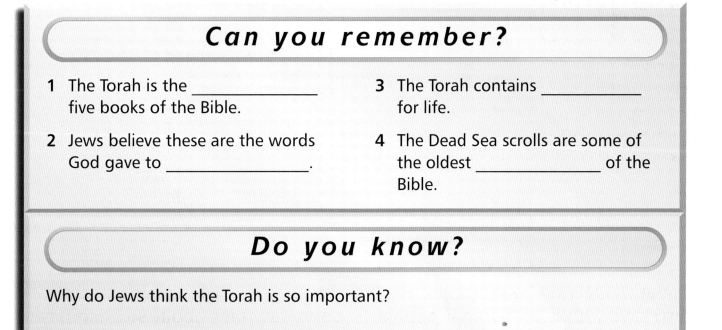

Can you remember?

1 The Torah is the _____ five books of the Bible.

2 Jews believe these are the words God gave to _____.

3 The Torah contains _____ for life.

4 The Dead Sea scrolls are some of the oldest _____ of the Bible.

Do you know?

Why do Jews think the Torah is so important?

A Torah scroll is shown a lot of **respect**. It is covered by a velvet cloth called a **mantle**. **Silver** objects can be hung in front to make it beautiful.

The silver label that hangs in front is called a breastplate. What is the shape in the centre of it? Look on page 44 to help you. The lions on it are an important symbol of Judaism.

The scroll is wound round two wooden rollers. On top are crowns. They show the Torah is important like a king.

A Torah scroll with its decorative covering on like this is called a dressed scroll.

Using the Torah

The scroll is carried high up when it is brought out to be read. Everybody can see the Torah.

The scroll is put on a desk in the middle of the synagogue to be read. This is on a raised platform so people can hear the Torah. It also shows that the word of God is above people.

A scroll is handwritten. People do not touch the writing with their finger in case it gets smudged. Then it would be hard to read. Instead they use a pointer called a **yad**.

A yad.

Can you remember?

1 A _____ is the name for the cover of a scroll.

2 The Torah scroll is shown great _____.

3 Objects made of _____ are hung on the scroll to make it look beautiful.

4 A _____ is used to stop the writing getting smudged.

Do you know?

How do Jews show respect for the word of God?

1.6 Extension tasks

1 **a)** What symbols of Judaism can you see in this picture?
b) Do you know what they mean?

2 • Draw the outline of these pieces of stone into your book.

• Look at the Ten Commandments in Exodus 20.1–18.
• Make up your own Ten Commandments for today and write them into the tablets in your book.

3 This is Hebrew writing. Write the word Shabbat in Hebrew in your book.

ט	ח	ז	ו	ה	ד	ג	ב	א
Tet	Chet	Zayin	Vav	He	Dalet	Gimel	Bet	Alef
(T)	(Ch)	(Z)	(V/O/U)	(H)	(D)	(G)	(B/V)	(Silent)

ס	ן	נ	ם	מ	ל	ך	כ	י
Samech	Nun	Nun	Mem	Mem	Lamed	Kahf	Kaf	Yod
(S)	(N)	(N)	(M)	(M)	(L)	(Kh)	(K/KH)	(Y)

ת	ש	ר	ק	ץ	צ	ף	פ	ע
Tav	Shin	Resh	Qof	Tzade	Tzade	Fe	Pe	Ayin
(T/S)	(Sh/S)	(R)	(Q)	(Tz)	(Tz)	(F)	(P/F)	(Silent)

Remember Hebrew is written from right to left. It does not use vowels, so leave the 'a' out.

4 Design your own menorah. It must have seven branches but can be whatever shape you like.

5

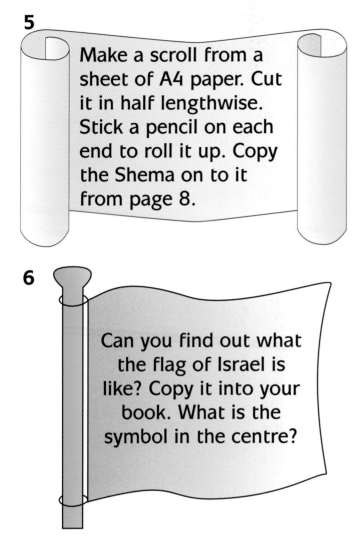

Make a scroll from a sheet of A4 paper. Cut it in half lengthwise. Stick a pencil on each end to roll it up. Copy the Shema on to it from page 8.

6

Can you find out what the flag of Israel is like? Copy it into your book. What is the symbol in the centre?

7 Use a Bible to work out this recipe below.

Ingredients:
1   150 grams Judges 5.25
2   150 grams Jeremiah 6.20
3   4 Jeremiah 17.11
4   225 grams 1 Samuel 30.12 (stoned)
5   225 grams Nahum 3.12 (chopped)

6   50 grams Numbers 17.8 (blanched and chopped)
7   275 grams 1 Kings 4.22
8   1 tsp 2 Chronicles 9.9
9   1 pinch Leviticus 2.13
10 ½ tsp Amos 4.5 (baking powder).

Method:
Beat 1 and 2 together. Add 3 one at a time still beating. Add 4, 5 and 6 and beat. Sieve 7, 8, 9 and 10 together and add to the mixture. Put in a 7" cake tin and bake for 2 hours at 150°C.

Caves at Qumran.

8 The Dead Sea scrolls were found in these caves. Can you find out how they were found? You could also look on the Internet to find out how scholars are getting on piecing some of the scrolls together.

17

2.1 Abraham

Who was Abraham?

Abraham founded Judaism. He did not believe in lots of gods. He thought there was only **one** God. Jews think God spoke to Abraham and told him to take his tribe to a new country.

Did Abraham exist?

Yes. There are some facts about this person that can be proved. Historians think he lived 4,000 years ago in Iraq. He was the head of a rich tribe. They lived in **tents** and moved around the country. Abraham's tribe would have owned many animals and moved to fresh land for them to graze.

His travels are told in Genesis. They can be plotted on a map. The tribe and their animals would have walked 1,400 miles. That is no mean feat! It took them many years. They travelled into Israel. In those days Israel was called Canaan. They also went down into Egypt.

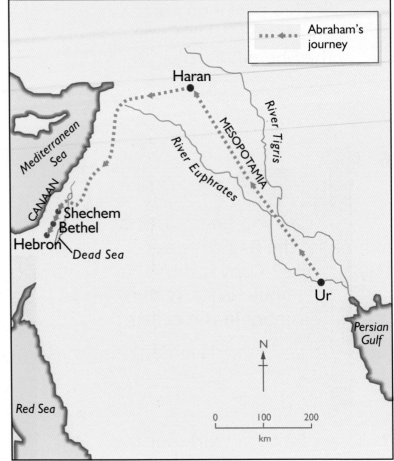

Why is Abraham important?

- He was the first person to believe in one God. God made the Covenant with him, see page 10.
- Jews call Abraham the **father** of Judaism. They think he was the ancestor of all Jews.
- He was the person who took the Jews to the land **God** promised them.
- He was the Jews' first teacher.

Today some people still live as Abraham did. They are called the Bedouin. The families own lots of animals. They move from place to place to find grazing for their sheep and goats. Their tents are often woven out of the wool from their goats.

This is a modern Bedouin camp.

Can you remember?

1 Abraham was different because he believed in _____ God.

2 Historians think he was the head of a rich tribe who lived in _____.

3 Jews think he is the _____ of Judaism.

4 Abraham took the Jews to the land _____ promised them.

Do you know?

What is the name for the people today who live in the same way as Abraham did?

2.2 Moses the leader

Hollywood hero?

Moses makes a great story! Several films have been made about his life like *Moses*, *The Ten Commandments* and the £75 million *The Prince of Egypt*. Here is a taste of the action:

- Moses was lost as a baby and found by a princess.
- He killed a soldier and went on the run.
- Moses met God and was sent back to help the Jews.
- He freed 600,000 people.
- Moses opened the Red Sea to let the Jews cross.
- He led crowds around for 40 years (with no maps!) and reached the **Promised** Land.

It is easy to see why Moses is a hero.

The Exodus

Jews think Moses is a good role model. He **trusted** in God totally. Moses took a great risk to set the Jews free. He asked the king to let the Jews go. The king refused. God sent ten **plagues** on the Egyptians. Read them in Exodus 7.14–11.9. Only when the king's own son died did he say the Jews could go. Moses led the people out. This is called the Exodus.

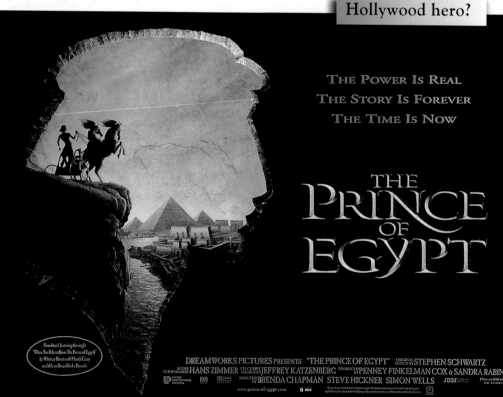

Hollywood hero?

THE POWER IS REAL
THE STORY IS FOREVER
THE TIME IS NOW

THE PRINCE OF EGYPT

DREAMWORKS PICTURES PRESENTS "THE PRINCE OF EGYPT" ORIGINAL SONGS BY STEPHEN SCHWARTZ
SCORE COMPOSED BY HANS ZIMMER EXECUTIVE PRODUCER JEFFREY KATZENBERG PRODUCED BY PENNEY FINKELMAN COX & SANDRA RABINS
DIRECTED BY BRENDA CHAPMAN STEVE HICKNER SIMON WELLS
www.prince-of-egypt.com

Is any of it true?

- Rameses II was King of Egypt when Moses was there.
- The disasters followed each other naturally.
- The Nile flooded and red mud carried deadly bugs in it.
- In 1997 fish were killed by a red bug in the USA and the water turned red.
- Frogs were poisoned and died on land.
- Flies ate the frogs. Flies' eggs spread the bugs to humans and animals.
- Locusts and hailstorms happened anyway.
- Eclipses make it dark.
- If food ran out in Egypt, they might cut the corn too early. Deadly bugs can then grow in the grain.
- They used to give the oldest son twice as much food at harvest time. He was poisoned.
- Graves from the time of Rameses II have lots of skeletons of boys.
- A storm could blow the Red Sea onto the land. Then the water would become shallow. People could walk across it. The water would rush back when the wind dropped.

We do not know if it happened like this. There are new ideas suggested all the time. Jews think Moses was a special person. God **chose** him to help the Jews escape.

Can you remember?

1 Moses _____ in God completely.

2 God sent ten _____ to force the king to let the Jews go.

3 Moses led the Jews to the _____ Land.

4 Jews think God _____ Moses as leader.

Do you know?

Why are so many films made about Moses' life?

2.3 Moses the teacher

On the move

Moses led the people and their animals a long way. They must have looked like the refugees we see on the television news. Look at the map and work out how far they went. They reached Sinai in seven weeks. Then they moved north and stayed in one place for 38 years. Finally they moved to the Promised Land, Israel.

Refugees on the move today.

Moses the organiser

Life was difficult for Moses. First the people moaned about everything – the food, the water and living conditions. Then everybody expected him to know the answers to their family problems. It was very tiring. He worked from early till late answering their questions. Then he trained others to do this.

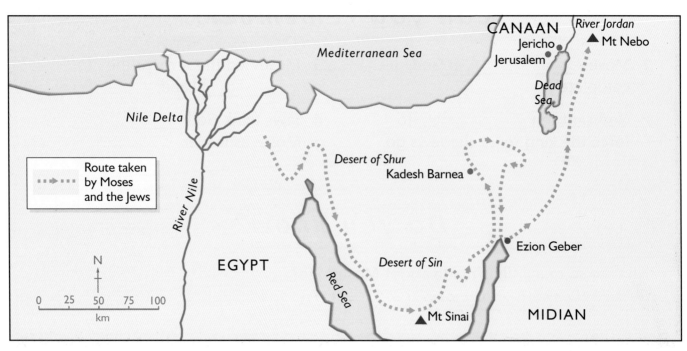

Giving of the Torah

On the map you can see they went to Mount **Sinai**. God told Moses to climb the mountain alone. Moses stayed on the mountain for 40 days. In that time God gave him the Ten Commandments and over 600 other rules for **living**.

Some Jews think every word God told Moses was written down carefully. No mistakes were made. These words filled five books. The books are called the **Torah**. This means the law. The Torah tells Jews exactly how to lead the sort of life God wants them to. The Torah is the most important writings the Jews have.

Why is Moses so important?

Moses is the greatest **messenger** in Judaism. God chose him to:
- lead the Jews to the Promised Land.
- give the people God's laws.

Moses made the Jews feel a united group. He taught them about God. Moses also gave them rules about living. The laws and ceremonies Moses set up are still in use today.

Muslims and Christians also think Moses was an important messenger.

Can you remember?

1 Moses was given the Torah on Mount _____.

2 The name _____ means the law.

3 God gave Moses the rules for _____.

4 Moses is the greatest _____ in Judaism.

Do you know?

What sort of things did Moses teach the Jews?

2.4 David, Solomon and the Temple

Moses worked hard to get the Jews to the Promised Land. But he never went there himself. He saw it from the top of a hill before he died. By then he was very old, over a hundred years old!

Battles

Life was not easy once the Jews arrived there. Other people lived in the country and did not want the Jews to take it. There were many battles. In one famous battle the giant Goliath was killed by David, one of the Jews. You may know this story. It is in 1 Samuel 17.41.

King David

David went on to become the king of the Jews. He was a great **war** hero and won the country for his people. But he also had to work hard to stop the Jews fighting amongst themselves. To help them

feel on the same side, David made the hill town of **Jerusalem** his capital. It became an important town. Jerusalem was also the centre of worship of the one God. David brought the Ten **Commandments** to Jerusalem.

This street entertainer is dressed up as King David. If you look up 1 Samuel 16.23 you can read why he plays a harp.

Solomon

When David died his son Solomon became king. The country was rich and peaceful. Solomon used the money to build a large **Temple**. Inside he put the two pieces of stone that Moses was given with the Ten Commandments on. The Temple was a very important centre of worship.

The destruction of the Temple

The Temple lasted for 400 years until invaders destroyed it. A new one was built on the same spot. It was the most holy place for Jews to worship. But the Romans destroyed this Temple in 70 CE. Today only one part of the wall remains.

This scale model of the second Temple was built from details in the scriptures.

Can you remember?

1 King David was a great _____ hero.

2 David made _____ the centre for worship.

3 The Ten _____ were brought to Jerusalem.

4 Solomon built a huge _____ to worship God.

Do you know?

Which part of the Temple can Jews visit today?

2.5 The Holocaust

Hate!

Today there are many terrible accounts of hatred in the news. Some countries try to get rid of people they do not want by killing them. Many others are chased out of the country they have always lived in.

This has happened to the Jews many times in their history. The worst time was between 1933 and 1945 in Germany. This is called the **Holocaust**. Hitler and the Nazis killed one **third** of all the Jews in the world.

The scapegoat

Hitler looked for somebody to blame for the Germans losing the First World War. A person who is made to take the blame is called a scapegoat. Hitler picked on the Jews. He said the Jews caused all the trouble. 'Germany must get rid of all the Jews', he said.

'It took between 3 to 15 minutes to kill the people in the death chamber, depending on the climatic conditions. We knew the people were dead because their screaming stopped.'
A Nazi soldier said this. He worked at a death camp that killed 6,000 people every day.

GRAVE Nº1
APPROX. 1,000
22ND APRIL 1945.

Judaism in history

Banned

Germans who were Jewish had their **rights** removed. If they owned a shop or factory, it was taken away. They were banned from using the swimming pools and libraries. They lost their jobs. Many were beaten up on the street. Jews tried to escape from Germany. But some of the countries they escaped to were soon taken over by the Nazis. The horrors began again.

Extermination

Hitler began to round up the Jews. They were put on trains and taken to death camps. They could not escape. Children, babies and old people were **gassed**. Others were worked to death or died of hunger.

At the end of the war, people saw sights like this picture opposite for the first time. They were shocked. Jews think it is important that people know about it. They say this sort of thing must never happen again in the world.

Britain remembers

In 2000 Britain set up a special Holocaust day. On 27 January every year people remember the Jews who were killed by the Nazis. It was that day at the end of the Second World War that the Jews were freed from Auschwitz death camp.

Page 82 tells you how the Holocaust is remembered today.

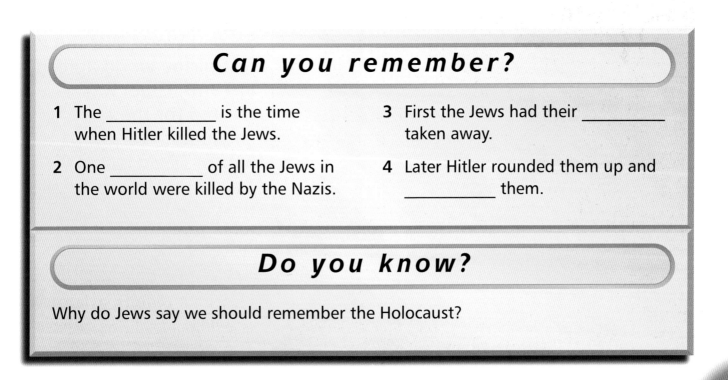

Can you remember?

1 The _____ is the time when Hitler killed the Jews.

2 One _____ of all the Jews in the world were killed by the Nazis.

3 First the Jews had their _____ taken away.

4 Later Hitler rounded them up and _____ them.

Do you know?

Why do Jews say we should remember the Holocaust?

2.6 The Promised Land

Jews think they should have their own country. God promised them a land of their own in the Covenant (see page 10). When the Jews first arrived in Israel with **Abraham**, God told them this land was theirs. Later God said if the Jews did not obey him, there would be wars. The Jews would be scattered all over the world. This has happened to the Jews many times.

Defeat

In the past the Romans took over Israel like they did Britain. The Jews tried to fight them off but failed. The **Romans** ended up smashing the Temple to pieces. They also persecuted the Jews. Many left Israel to avoid being killed. They went to other parts of the world. Their families settled there and never returned. Today more Jews live outside Israel than in it.

Setting up the state of Israel

The Jews have suffered a great deal in their history. The Holocaust was the worst time. Jews felt there would only be peace if they had their own country. After the Second World War the rest of the world agreed. In **1948**, Israel was created for the Jews. It had a new flag with a Star of David (see page 7) and the stripes from the prayer shawl (see page 49).

Some Jews in Israel wear a nineteenth-century style of clothing.

A haven

One of the first laws Israel created gave anyone who was Jewish the right to live in the country. Some Jews returned because their roots were there. Other Jews have moved to Israel because they were being attacked.

Modern Israel

Not all Jews in Israel are **religious**. Some are Jewish by birth but think the rules in the Torah need to be adapted for modern times. Others say the rules must be strictly followed. People don't always agree over this.

Dana International, won the Eurovision Song Contest for Israel. Strict Jews were angry about this. The rehearsals took place on a holy day and Dana, who was born a man, had undergone a sex change.

Can you remember?

1 God told _____ that Israel was the land promised to the Jews.

2 The _____ smashed the Jews' Temple to pieces.

3 Modern Israel was set up in _____ after the Second World War.

4 Not all Jews in Israel are _____.

Do you know?

Why were some Jews angry when Dana won the Eurovision Song Contest?

2.7 Extension tasks

1 Write a newspaper report about the plagues. This is the headline.

**North Egypt declared disaster zone!
Pharaoh asks for aid!**

2

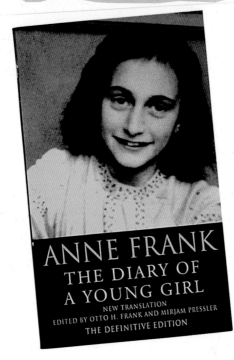

This girl above is called Anne Frank. When the Nazis came, she hid with her family in an attic. Anne kept a diary. Can you find out about her life? You may be able to get this book in the library.

3

Role play. In pairs act out:
- either a scene when Moses asks the king of Egypt to let the Jews go free.
- or a scene between Moses and one of the Jews. They are in the desert. The Jew is moaning. He is hungry and tired and wants to know why they ever left Egypt.

4

Design a poster to advertise a film about King David. You can make up your own title for the film.

5

    a) What country was Abraham born in?

    b) How did Abraham and his family travel?

    c) Why did Abraham move his tribe around?

6

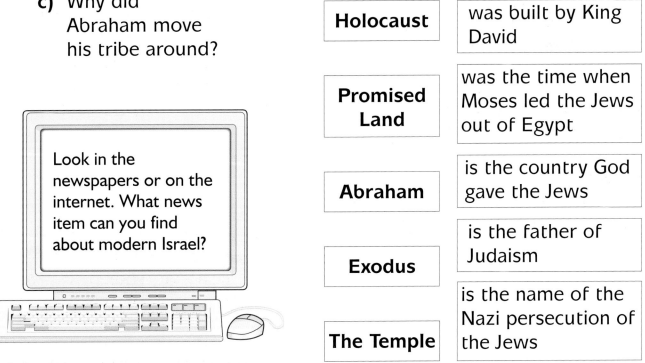

Look in the newspapers or on the internet. What news item can you find about modern Israel?

7 Write two sentences to go under this picture of the Holocaust.

8 Copy down each word on the left. Find the correct meaning on the right. Write it by the side to finish each sentence.

Holocaust	was built by King David
Promised Land	was the time when Moses led the Jews out of Egypt
Abraham	is the country God gave the Jews
Exodus	is the father of Judaism
The Temple	is the name of the Nazi persecution of the Jews

3.1 Family life

A clever Jewish teacher said this when someone asked him where God was. People were surprised. They thought he would say 'go to the synagogue'. Jews think the **home** and family are the centre of their religion.

Where did you learn?

Where did you learn most about life? At school? Or at home? Most people would say at home. We spend more time at home than at school. And we learn from our parents, friends and other people we mix with. Jews believe Judaism is a way of **life**, not just a religion. So home plays a really important part.

The duties of parents

Jewish parents believe they should love and care for their children. But they also think they should teach them life skills. 'Teach your son a trade, or you teach him to become a robber' it says in their scriptures. Jewish parents have a duty to ensure their children behave themselves until a boy is 13 years old and a girl is 12 years old.

The duties of children

Children have a duty to their parents. The Ten Commandments say 'Honour your father and mother'. Children must respect their parents all their life.

In the home

There are many reminders of God in the home. A small box

Jews believe family life is a vital part of the religion.

containing a prayer is fixed to the front door of a Jewish house. Jews prepare their food following the rules in the Torah. A **blessing** is said before the family eat to thank God for the food.

One day a week is a holy day. It is a day for resting with the family and studying the Torah.

Everyone enjoys the Jewish **festivals** and these are very much a part of home life. Special foods remind people of their Jewish past. Children learn stories about their history.

The Jewish mother

Jews think the mother has a special part to play in family life.

The children will learn most about their religion at home from her. Strict Jews believe you can only be Jewish if you have a Jewish mother. Other Jews say you are Jewish if either parent is a Jew. All Jews think they should marry and have children to keep the religion alive.

On Saturday morning Jewish families try to attend synagogue together for worship.

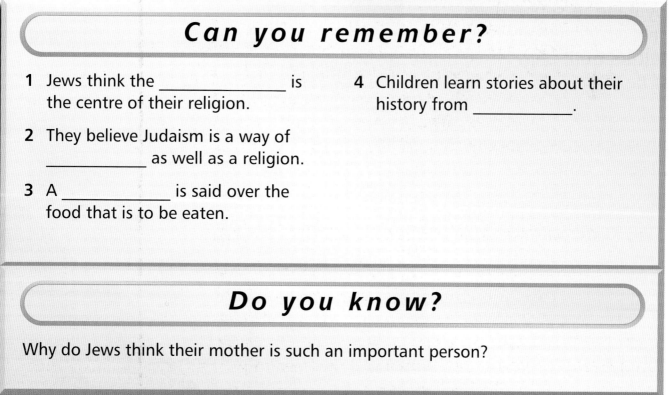

Can you remember?

1 Jews think the _____ is the centre of their religion.

2 They believe Judaism is a way of _____ as well as a religion.

3 A _____ is said over the food that is to be eaten.

4 Children learn stories about their history from _____.

Do you know?

Why do Jews think their mother is such an important person?

3.2 Mezuzah

What is it?

A mezuzah is a piece of parchment. It has the **Shema** prayer written on it (see page 8). The parchment scroll is put in a case and nailed to the **door-frame** of a Jewish home.

Why?

Jews do this because the Torah says they must write the Shema on their door-frame. They put it in a case so the rain will not wash the ink off.

The scroll inside is written by hand. A scribe does this very carefully with a **quill** pen. If he makes a mistake he must scrape the letter off. But if he writes the name of God wrongly, he must start all over again. Jews say God's name is too holy to be scratched off.

The case can be made of anything like wood, plastic or metal. Jews touch the case as they go inside the home. They may also kiss their finger-tips to show their respect for God. The mezuzah reminds them that God is in the **house**. God will look after them when they go out and when they come in. They must keep God's rules.

A mezuzah showing the Shema written on parchment. It is taken out and checked for damage every seven years.

House-warming

Jews like to fix a mezuzah to their house as soon as they move in. It is a good excuse for a house-warming party! Some shops and offices have a mezuzah on their doors as well. But they do not have to. The Torah says it is the places where people live that need a mezuzah.

The Hebrew letters spell 'Almighty', one of the names for God.

Can you Remember?

1 A mezuzah case has the _____ prayer inside.

2 The mezuzah case is fixed to the _____ of a Jewish home.

3 The scribe writes the Shema by hand with a _____ pen.

4 The mezuzah reminds Jews that God is in the _____.

Do you know?

When would a scribe have to re-write a scroll?

3.3 Kosher rules

Would you eat anything?

'I could eat a horse!' But would you? What about fried slug? There are many things we can eat but choose not to.

Someone may be vegetarian because:

- they were brought up that way.
- they care about animals.
- they think it is healthy.
- they don't like the taste of meat.

These chocolate biscuits are marked kosher. K = kosher D = dairy. LBD is the London Bet Din, the court of rabbis who inspect the biscuits.

We eat to live. We don't live to eat!

People say we are not like animals. We do have to eat to live. But we don't just gobble up food like a dog. People take care choosing and cooking their food. Meals are set out carefully. By taking care with our food, Jews think we are controlling our basic instinct. We can move from the animal towards God.

God gave Moses rules about food. The rules are called **kosher** rules. Kosher means correct. The Jews were told to keep the rules as part of the Covenant. The rules were needed in the past to teach the Jews how to keep healthy. Today Jews still keep those rules because God gave them. They also think that keeping the kosher rules **unites** them as a group. It is a bit like friends choosing to wear the same trainers.

Three basic kosher rules:

- blood must not be eaten in meat.

A joint of meat is soaked in salt water. Then it is rinsed and cooked. This removes the blood.

- only certain animals can be eaten.

The Torah tells Jews what sort of meat they can eat:
- animals must have a parted hoof and chew the cud.
- birds must be farmed.
- fish must have fins and scales.

- meat and **milk** must not be mixed in a meal.

The **Torah** says that meat and milk cannot be eaten in the same meal. Jews have to remember which foods contain milk. That may be cheese, cream or chocolate.

Eggs, fish, vegetables and cereal can be eaten with anything kosher.

Can you remember?

1 The food rules are called the _____ rules.

2 The rules about what is correct to eat are in the _____.

3 Obeying the same rules _____ the Jews.

4 Meat and _____ cannot be eaten in the same meal.

Do you know?

Why do Jews today think they must keep these rules?

שַׁבָּת שָׁלוֹם

Shabbat Shalom!

This means 'peaceful Shabbat' in Hebrew. Jews look forward to Shabbat on Friday night. It is a day for everyone to have a **rest**. Nobody has to go to work or school. They have 24 hours as a family. There is a special family meal Friday evening.

Blessing the wine
Wine means joy in Judaism. Jews are happy that they have a day when they are free from work. They remember God rested on the seventh day after he created the **world**. The father blesses the **wine**. He takes a sip and gives it to everyone else to taste.

Can you remember?

1 Shabbat is a day for Jews to have a _____.

2 Jews remember God rested after the creation of the _____.

3 Shabbat starts with the blessing over two _____ before sunset.

4 The father shares _____ and bread with everyone.

Do you know?

What does the bread on the Shabbat table remind Jews of?

Lighting the Shabbat candles
Just before sunset the woman lights two **candles**. These are a sign of joy and warmth. She says a blessing as she lights the candles.

Two loaves of bread
The two loaves of bread are like the food God gave Moses and the Jews in the desert. The father says a blessing over the bread. Then he breaks some off to give to everybody. They eat it. Then they will eat their evening meal.

Shabbat starts at sunset on Friday. It lasts until sunset on Saturday.

No electricity

In the Torah Jews are told to **rest** on Shabbat because God rested on the seventh day after creating the world. There is a list of work Jews are told not to do on Shabbat. One job is not to light a fire. Today Jews say this means they must not use **electricity** because it needs a spark. They do not drive cars either on Shabbat.

Have a rest

Non-Jews might think this is terrible. But Jews say it is freedom. You do not have to go to work or do any jobs at home. And no homework! This is a time for the **family** and for the Torah.

Havdalah

At **sunset** on Saturday the family gather together. They have a ceremony to end the holy day. This is called Havdalah. The father says four blessings.

- The first is said over a cup of wine meaning joy.
- The second is said over a spice box to hope for a good week.
- The third is said over a candle with many wicks. This shows they can now light fire again.
- The last blessing is said when the candle is snuffed out. Thanks are given for Shabbat.

The family get together on Shabbat.

Havdalah

Can you remember?

1 Shabbat is a day of _____.

2 Jews spend the day with their _____ and the Torah.

3 They do not use _____ on Shabbat.

4 At _____ on Saturday there is a ceremony to end Shabbat.

Do you know?

Why don't Jews use their cars on Shabbat?

3.6 Extension tasks

1 Try this role play in pairs:
Act out a scene between a
Jewish teenager and his mum.
The teenager wants to go to a
disco on Shabbat. His mum
wants him to stay home for the
Shabbat meal.

2

Kosher restaurant opening soon!

In groups of three or four plan
the opening of this new
restaurant.
- Work out a Jewish name.
- Plan some kosher menus –
  you could have kosher Indian,
  or kosher Chinese if you like.
- Design a poster to advertise
  the new restaurant. Include
  some menus and costs.

3 Fold an A4 sheet of paper to
make a leaflet. Call it HELPFUL
TIPS FOR SHABBAT. The leaflet
will be useful if a person is
invited to stay with a Jewish
family for the weekend but is
not Jewish him/herself.
- Inside the leaflet explain
  what happens on Friday
  night.
- Tell the person what to
  expect on Saturday.
- You can include sketches or
  diagrams that might be
  helpful.

4 Copy out the three true
sentences below.
a) A Jewish mother is a very
important person in
Judaism.
b) You are Jewish if you have a
Jewish dad.
c) The mezuzah is eaten every
Saturday.
d) Jews cannot drive to
synagogue on a Saturday.
e) A cheeseburger is not
kosher.

5

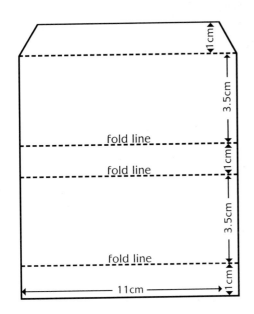

Make a mezuzah case
- Draw an outline of the mezuzah case on a piece of paper or thin card. Remember to include a tab along the edge to stick the case together.
- Cut out and fold along the creases.
- Inside the case write the Shema (see page 8).
- Decorate the front of the case with Jewish symbols.
- Glue the tab.

6

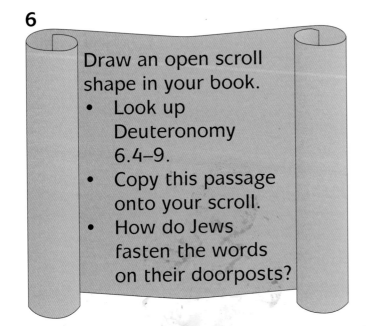

Draw an open scroll shape in your book.
- Look up Deuteronomy 6.4–9.
- Copy this passage onto your scroll.
- How do Jews fasten the words on their doorposts?

7 Make a poster to show what happens at Havdalah. Jews say this ceremony includes the five senses. The candle's warmth is touch. What do you think the other senses are?

8

This is a picture of the first McDonald's to open in Israel. What changes do you think they had to make for the food to be kosher?

4.1 Synagogue

The Ten Commandments are carved on two pieces of **stone**. They are written in Hebrew. There is a **lamp** hanging in front. It is kept alight all the time to show God is always present. There used to be a lamp like this in the first Temple.

The ark is the holiest place in the synagogue. This cupboard has two doors and a curtain so the Torah **scrolls** are kept safely inside. The ark is raised to show respect for God's word. It is found on the wall facing Jerusalem.

Can you remember?

1 The ark is important because it contains the _____.

2 Two pieces of _____ have the Ten Commandments carved on them.

3 A _____ is kept alight to show God is always there.

4 Men and women sit apart in some synagogues so they do not get _____.

Do you know?

Which place does the ark face?

In this synagogue men and women sit apart so they will not be **distracted**. The men sit at ground level and the women upstairs. Children can sit with either parent.

4.2 The synagogue community

Synagogue means **meeting** place. It is an important centre for the Jews in the area because it is:

- a social centre. In the hall nearby, people go to youth clubs and classes. Wedding receptions can be held there.

- a place of worship. Services are on Monday, Thursday and on Shabbat.

- a place of learning. There is a **library**. Groups meet to study the Torah. Children go to classes on Sunday.

Rabbi

Rabbi means **teacher**. He is not a priest. Jews do not need a rabbi to have a service in the synagogue.

The rabbi helps with worship by:
- leading the prayers.
- reading the weekly piece of Torah.
- giving a sermon on Shabbat.

The rabbi cares for people by:
- visiting Jews in hospital, prison or at home if they are ill.
- helping with marriage problems.
- talking to people after someone has died.
- conducting weddings and funerals.

The rabbi teaches:
- the meaning of the Torah.
- rules for everyday living.

Scribe

A scribe does not work in the synagogue. But he does write the scrolls that are used there. It is an important job because there must be no **mistakes** in the word of God.

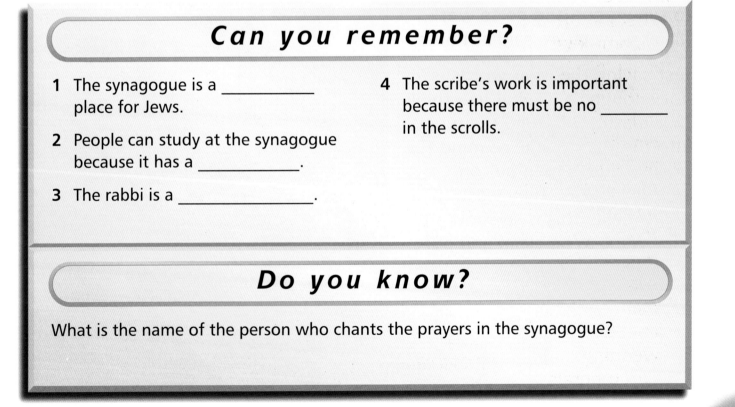

Cantor

The cantor leads the worship by singing. No musical instruments are used on Shabbat. He stands in the centre of the synagogue to chant the prayers and readings from the Torah. It is easy to see a cantor because he wears a tall hat.

Can you remember?

1 The synagogue is a _____ place for Jews.

2 People can study at the synagogue because it has a _____.

3 The rabbi is a _____.

4 The scribe's work is important because there must be no _____ in the scrolls.

Do you know?

What is the name of the person who chants the prayers in the synagogue?

4.3 Prayer

Is prayer important?

Jews think prayer is a way of **talking** to God. They can pray at any time and anywhere. Some people like to pray alone. If they choose to pray as a group, ten men are needed for a service. Women are not included because they do not have to say the same prayers as men.

Daily prayer

Jewish men pray in the **morning**, afternoon and evening like their early leaders did. It is not always easy to go to synagogue and go to work. Many prayers are said at home.

Just saying the right words is not enough. It is what you think that matters. To help them get into the right frame of mind for prayer, Jewish men put on special clothes. They wash their hands next. This is to show that they want to be clean and pure.

Praying in the open air

These women are praying outside at a wall that was part of the old Temple. Some read from a prayer book. Others make up their own prayer. Some write one on paper and tuck it into the cracks in the wall.

Prayer can take place outside.

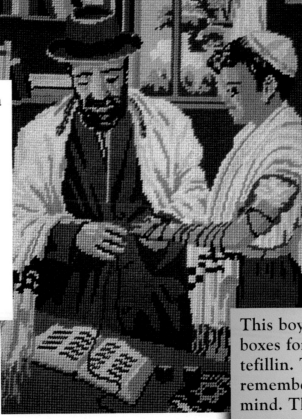

The shawl is called a **tallit**. It is worn for morning prayer. When a Jewish man puts it round him, he remembers God wraps love around him. There is one tassel for each of the commandments a Jew must keep.

This cap is called a **kippah**. It is worn for prayer to show God is above people. Some boys and men wear one all day to show God respect.

This boy wears two black leather boxes for prayer. They are called tefillin. The one on the head is to remember to worship God with the mind. The one strapped on the arm, near the heart, reminds him to love God with all his strength.

Can you remember?

1 Prayer is a way of _____ to God.

2 Jews pray in the _____, afternoon and evening.

3 A _____ reminds a Jew that God is above him.

4 The prayer shawl is called a _____.

Do you know?

Why do Jews take time to put on these special clothes?

4.4 Extension tasks

1 What do the arrows point to in the picture of the inside of a synagogue.

2 The synagogue in the new town of Sherton needs a rabbi. Their present one is retiring. Write an advert to go in *The Jewish Star Weekly*. Say what sort of things the rabbi will have to do.

3 Fold an A4 sheet of paper to make a leaflet. This is to be given to the people who might visit the synagogue in the picture above.
   • Explain the most important things they will see.
   • A floor plan or some sketches may be helpful.

4

This is a photograph of the Chief Rabbi in Britain. Can you find out his name?

5 Match the word to its meaning:

Tallit	the cupboard where the scrolls are kept.
Cantor	a cap worn by men for prayers.
Ark	a prayer shawl.
Kippah	the person who chants the prayers.

6

Make a poster that could be pinned up outside the synagogue. Choose one of the activities that might take place in the week. Decorate it with some symbols of Judaism.

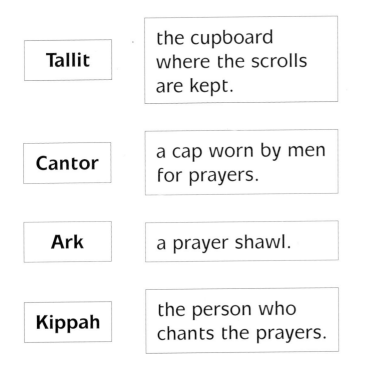

7 Role play
Try this in pairs. A teacher is trying to arrange work experience for a Year 10 pupil with a Jewish scribe. What will the scribe say about the work he does?

8 a) When must Jewish men pray?
b) Where are tefillin worn?
c) How can you tell who is the cantor in the synagogue?

5.1 Birth ceremonies

The whole world rejoices when a baby is born.

Jews think children are a **gift** from God. By having children people are taking part in creation. So everyone is happy when a baby is born.

The birth of a girl

After a baby girl is born, her **father** is called up to stand by the Torah when it is read. He says a blessing over the scroll and tells everyone the little girl's name. There is a family party afterwards.

The birth of a boy

Eight days after a boy is born, there is a family party. People are happy the baby is well and want to keep the promise God made to Abraham. This promise is called the Covenant.

In Genesis God told Abraham to **circumcise** every baby boy at **eight** days old. This means the foreskin is cut from the penis by a trained Jew.

This can take place at home, in hospital or in a room at the synagogue.

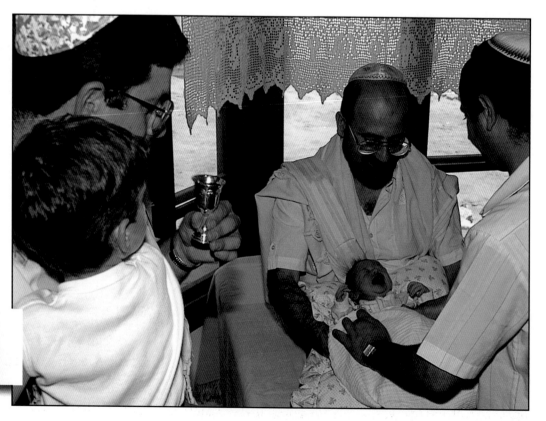

A baby boy is circumcised at eight days old.

A family friend is chosen to hold the baby on his lap during the operation. A blessing is said over the baby. Wine is blessed. The baby has a few drops put on his tongue. Then his father says his name. A bandage is put on the baby's wound. He heals in a few days. The baby is handed back to his mum.

Names

Babies are given a special Jewish name as well as their normal one. This is used in synagogue or at their wedding. It is often a name from the Bible. Some Jews are given the name of a favourite person in their family who has died.

This is called Elijah's chair. The person holding the baby during the circumcision sits here.

Can you remember?

1 Babies are a _____ from God.

2 The _____ names a baby girl at the synagogue.

3 God told Jews to _____ baby boys.

4 The ceremony for a little boy is carried out when he is _____ days old.

Do you know?

Why did God tell the Jews to circumcise their baby boys? (Page 10 will help you.)

5.2 Bar and Bat Mitzvah

THE BOY: **Today I am a man.**

HIS FATHER: **Blessed is the One who has freed me from responsibility for the boy's sins.**

Getting ready

Jews like to have a ceremony in the **synagogue** to mark this important step. It is called **Bar Mitzvah** in Hebrew. Before the ceremony the boy has to learn to read in Hebrew from the scrolls. He also learns about prayer and his religion.

Taking over

There are 613 rules in Judaism. **Children** are not expected to keep them all. When a boy is 13 years old he is thought to be mature enough to keep the rules himself. Before that his **father** has to watch over him.

The ceremony

This is held on Shabbat after his thirteenth birthday. All the boy's family who have watched him grow up will be there. They are proud to see him read from the Torah. This can be very scary but there is a big family party afterwards.

The boy reads the scrolls in Hebrew.

A girl's ceremony

Having a ceremony for a girl is a new idea. In the past they did not have one because women do not have to keep all the rules like the men. But women have different religious duties in the home. Girls wanted a ceremony to show they were now old enough to begin these. They can have a ceremony in the synagogue called Bat Mitzvah if they wish. Girls are said to mature before boys so it is held when they are 12 years old. There can be a small family party afterwards.

A girl is 12 years old when she has her Bat Mitzvah.

Can you remember?

1 _____ do not have to keep all 613 rules in Judaism.

2 The _____ is responsible for his son's behaviour until the boy is old enough.

3 The ceremony for a boy of 13 years is called _____ _____.

4 All the family come to watch the boy read in the _____.

Do you know?

Why do girls have their Bat Mitzvah a year before the boys?

5.3 Marriage

Marriage is a duty!

Jews think God has a plan for people to take part in **creation**. They believe all Jews should marry and have children. Making a new family is important to carry on the religion. Home is where people learn about religion and everyday life, so a Jew needs to marry another Jew.

Getting ready

An engaged couple first talk to the rabbi. He teaches them about Jewish family life. The wedding can talk place **anywhere**, only a canopy is needed and two witnesses. The canopy is called a **huppah**. It symbolises the new home the couple will make. The sides are open to show all will be welcomed.

Order of ceremony

- The grooms waits under the huppah for his bride.
- The bride comes in with her parents.
- The couple meet under the huppah.
- The **rabbi** blesses the wine. The couple each take a sip.
- The groom puts a ring on the bride's finger and says a blessing.
- The marriage contract is read. The bride, groom and two witnesses sign it.
- Seven blessings are sung.
- The groom is asked to stamp on an empty wine glass. This reminds people of the Temple that was destroyed. It also shows marriage can have good and bad times.
- Everybody shouts 'Mazel Tov!' This means 'Good luck!' in Hebrew.

The groom wears his tallit as he stands under the huppah with the bride and their parents. On the ground in front is a white cloth wrapped around the wine glass which the groom has just stamped on. The rabbi faces the congregation.

Can you remember?

1 Jews should marry to help God with _____.

2 The _____ is the Hebrew name for the marriage canopy.

3 Jews can get married _____ so long as there is a huppah and two witnesses.

4 The _____ takes the service.

Do you know?

Why does the bridegroom stamp on a wine glass?

5.4 Death, funerals and mourning

Jewish view of death

Jews think life and death are part of God's plan. They also believe in life **after** death. But Jews say life is for the living. There is no point in focusing on what might happen next.

Care of the dying

Jews take care of someone who is dying. They sit with them to give comfort. They may also help the dying person to say the **Shema** prayer.

After death the body is washed. It is wrapped in a plain cloth and put into a simple coffin. A man will have his **tallit**, the prayer shawl, put round his shoulders.

A dead person is never left on their own before they are buried. The funeral takes place soon after death.

The funeral

This is held at the cemetery, not in the synagogue. A special prayer and blessings are said at the graveside. Relatives make a tear in their clothes as a sign that they are torn apart by sadness.

Everyone shovels some soil into the grave. This makes them aware that the person really is dead.

A gravestone is put up to mark the grave and show the person is not forgotten. It is traditional for those who visit the grave to place a stone, rather than flowers, on it.

Mourning

For the first seven days the family stays at home and does nothing. Friends will come in and look after them. This gives the family time to **grieve**. Then they slowly get back into normal life over the next 21 days. No one goes out enjoying themselves until this time is past.

Children say a special prayer for a dead parent every day in the first year.

On the anniversary of a death, relatives light a Yahrzeit candle. This memorial candle burns for 25 hours.

Can you remember?

1 Jews believe in life _____ death but say you should concentrate on living.

2 A dying person tries to say the _____ prayer.

3 A man will be wrapped in his _____ in the coffin.

4 The family has seven days to _____ at home after a funeral.

Do you know?

Why do members of the family make a tear in their clothes at a funeral?

5.5 Extension tasks

1 Use a Bible to look up Hebrew names. Find five boys' names and five girls' names that are used today. Can you find out what any of them mean?

2

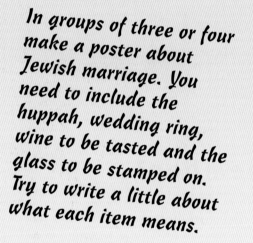

In groups of three or four make a poster about Jewish marriage. You need to include the huppah, wedding ring, wine to be tasted and the glass to be stamped on. Try to write a little about what each item means.

3 Do you think it is a good idea to let people have a long time to get over someone's death? How long should someone have off school if their granny dies?

4 Look at this Bar Mitzvah card. Write a sentence about each thing the arrow is pointing to.

5 In pairs try this role play between a Jewish father and a radio interviewer. The father tells the interviewer what happens at a boy's Brit Milah. The interviewer asks why Jewish boys are circumcised.

6 What do you think is put in the alcove of these graves on the anniversary of the death?

7 Draw a Yahrzeit candle. What is it used for? Why do you think people choose a candle?

8 Copy out the three correct sentences below.

a) A dying person hopes to say the Shema prayer.

b) Jews spend lots of money on funerals.

c) Stones are put on graves instead of flowers.

d) Jews say you should think more about living than dying.

e) The coffin is taken to the synagogue.

9 Look at this wedding photograph. Write a letter from the bride to her friend telling her about this wedding ceremony.

6.1 Passover preparations

Who passed over what?

Passover is the most important festival for Jews. It reminds them of the time God helped them escape from Egypt. You can look back to page 20 for the story. At that time the angel of death **passed** over the houses of the Jews but went into the houses of the Egyptians and killed their sons.

Jews remember this event as a time when **God** looked after them. God kept his side of the Covenant. They must keep theirs. Having a festival is a good way of teaching children their history.

Spring-cleaning

Passover is a spring festival and many people clean out their houses after the winter. For Jews this spring-cleaning has a special meaning. When the Jews were escaping from the Egyptians, God told them not to put yeast in their bread. If you make bread with yeast, you have to wait for it to rise. The Jews did not have time.

Today Jews remember this by clearing all the **yeast** from their houses for the week of Passover. Yeast is in many foods that have been made with flour. But it is also in things like beer and whisky.

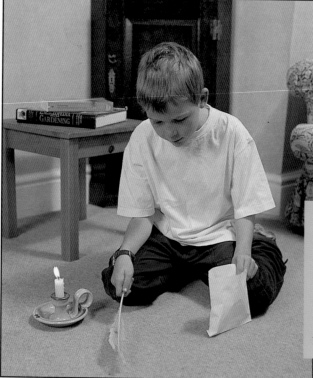

During the evening before Passover it is traditional for children to go searching for large crumbs with a feather, a candle and a bag. The crumbs have been hidden round the house by their parents. The finders get rewards!

Out with the yeast!

All the **cupboards** are emptied. The contents of each packet are read and checked. If there is any yeast in them, they will be put away until the end of Passover. In their place, Jews buy new packets that have never had contact with yeast. They are marked 'Kosher for Passover'.

Matzos contain no yeast. They taste like cracker biscuits.

RAKUSEN'S

TRADITIONAL

MATZOS

are certified as Kosher for Passover by the London Beth Din and the Ecclesiastical Authorities listed on the Seal. The products are made under Orthodox Rabbinical Supervision from the milling of the wheat to the sealing of the packet.
The Matzos are produced to the most stringent standards to meet the requirements of religious law and modern food hygiene regulations.

5 010112 001548

INSTANT CASH WIN!

a gift at Passover

Norwood Ravenswood

RAKUSEN'S

TRADITIONAL

MATZOS

Contains *14* Matzos

98% FAT FREE   300g

KOSHER FOR PASSOVER

Actual Size

Can you remember?

1 This festival is called Passover because the angel of death _____ over the houses of the Jews.

2 At Passover Jews remember how _____ has looked after them.

3 Jews do not eat _____ in their bread at Passover.

4 Today Jews clean their _____ out at Passover.

Do you know?

Why do Jews buy new packets of food at Passover?

6.2 Passover meal

The Seder

Everybody looks forward to Passover evening. There is a big family celebration. The table is laid with a white cloth and special foods. All the things on the table have a meaning. Everyone has a copy of the **prayer** book.

When the family is sitting down, the youngest child stands up. He or she has to ask, 'Why is this night different from all other nights?' Then the father can tell the story of the Jews getting out of Egypt. He uses the things on the table to help him.

Afterwards the family enjoys a big supper with wine. At the end of the meal some matzos are shared. These are pieces of bread made without yeast. Some blessings are said. Wine is drunk. The evening ends singing favourite songs.

The meal begins when the candles are lit.

Can you remember?

1 Everybody has a _____ book to follow the Passover service.

2 Wine is drunk to celebrate their _____ from slavery.

3 Jews put special foods on the _____ plate on the table.

4 A green vegetable like _____ is used to mean freshness and hope.

Do you know?

Why do the Jews hope Elijah will return to earth again?

Three pieces of flat bread made without yeast are eaten. They remind Jews of the time when they had to escape from Egypt in a hurry.

Wine is to celebrate **freedom**. One extra glass is put out for the prophet Elijah. It is said he will return one day to start a peaceful age in the world. Some Jews open their front door at Passover in the hope he will come in.

The **Seder** plate has foods with special meanings. Many will not be eaten.
• A roasted lamb bone for the lamb killed at the first Passover.
• An egg means new life. It is specially toasted.
• Bitter herbs remember the harsh times.
• Salt water for the tears the slaves cried.
• **Lettuce** means freshness and hope.
• A sweet paste for the sweetness of freedom.

6.3 Hanukkah

The Festival of Lights

This is a favourite festival for Jews. It is called the Festival of Lights because it is in the **winter** and uses lots of candles. The festival is based on a story from Jewish history. But the story has an up-to-date meaning.

Judas the Hammer

A long time ago a Syrian king ruled the Jews. He would not let them follow their religion. Some Jews were killed, others hid in the hills. Their leader was Judas, nicknamed the **Hammer**! He helped the Jews to defeat the Syrian army and win their country back again.

The Temple Menorah

The Jews returned to their Temple. It was in a bad state so they cleaned it. They tried to light the menorah. There was only enough oil for one day but they lit it and sent for more oil. By a miracle the menorah stayed alight until the new oil came **eight** days later.

Jews think this is a sign that their religion will stay alive even in difficult times.

The nine-branched menorah is called a hanukkiah. Can you see the servant candle?

Let's celebrate!

Today Hanukkah lasts for eight days. Jews have a special menorah with eight candles on it and an extra one in the middle used to light the others. Children get presents and people send cards. Food cooked in oil like doughnuts and chips are eaten.

The little person can beat the bully!

Jews think this story means that the bully doesn't always win. It also reminds them that God will always help them as he has done many times in history. They also want to **dedicate** their lives to God like the Jews dedicated their Temple again.

This hanukkiah is in San Francisco. Which night of Hanukkah was the photograph taken? (Don't count the servant candle.)

Can you remember?

1 The festival of Hanukkah comes in the _____ months.

2 Jews remember the story about how Judas the _____ defeated their enemies.

3 The Temple Menorah burnt for _____ days when there was only enough oil for one day.

4 At Hanukkah Jews _____ their lives to God.

Do you know?

Why do Jews like the festival of Hanukkah?

6.4 Rosh Hashanah and Yom Kippur

Making a fresh start

Lots of people make a fresh start at New Year. Some make plans to keep fit or to keep up with their homework.

Rosh Hashanah is the name of the Jewish **New** Year. It is a time to celebrate creation, the start of the world. Jews enjoy sending each other cards for New Year and sharing a meal together. They use honey to symbolise their hope for a sweet new year. Apples are also popular at this time because the round shape is the hope for a full year, not cut short by death.

This is a serious time. Jews think about everything they have done **wrong** during the year. They hope God will forgive them.

Sound the shofar!

Jews try to go to synagogue at this time of the year. There they will hear the **shofar** blown many times. This is a ram's horn. In the past it was used to call people to war. Today it calls the Jews to say sorry to God for the wrong things they have done.

The shofar is made from a ram's horn.

Ten days

It is hard to put everything right overnight. Jews have ten days at New Year to:

- think about what they have done wrong.
- be sorry and try to put things right.
- accept other people's apologies.

Yom Kippur

This means the day when people are sorry for their sins. To show God they really are sorry, Jews **fast**. They do not eat or drink for 25 hours. The day is spent praying, reading and quietly thinking about God.

At synagogue

Many Jews spend the day at the synagogue. Some wear white to show they want to be free of sin. Inside the synagogue the scrolls and ark are dressed in white. At sunset the shofar is blown for the last time.

Jews spend much of Yom Kippur in prayer at the synagogue.

Can you remember?

1 Rosh Hashanah is Jewish _____ Year.

2 It is a time when Jews think about things they have done _____.

3 In the synagogue they will hear the _____ blown.

4 Jews _____ at Yom Kippur to show God they are sorry.

Do you know?

Why do you think Yom Kippur is the holiest day of the year for Jews?

Sukkot

This hut, called a sukkah, is built in a Jewish garden for the autumn festival of Sukkot.

Camping in the sukkah

The Torah says Jews must live in one of these little huts for the eight days of **Sukkot**. But it can rain hard in the autumn in Britain so many Jews just eat their meals there.

The huts are like the ones the early Jews had to live in when they escaped from Egypt. They depended on God to keep them safe.

Sukkot is a **harvest** festival. The ceiling of the hut has fruit and paper chains hung on it. The roof is made of tree branches so you can see the stars. Jews hope it will not rain at Sukkot!

Wave the lulav!

In the Torah Jews are told to pick certain plants at Sukkot. Today they make a lulav. This is made with a branch of palm, myrtle and willow. They are held in the right hand and waved all round. This shows God's blessings go everywhere. At the same time Jews hold a fruit in their left hand.

Sukkot is a happy time. Friends and families meet to share meals in the sukkah. Dairy foods are eaten at this time.

The lulav is made of a branch of palm, myrtle and willow.

Purim

Purim is an excuse to wear fancy dress, eat, drink and be merry. But it does have a serious message.

Carnival at the synagogue!

You do not think people would dress like this at **synagogue**! They also behave a bit wildly during the readings from the scrolls. Some boo and stamp when the baddy's name is read out.

The story is about a brave woman called **Esther**. She saved the lives of many Jews. Her story is in the Book of Esther. It makes exciting reading.

Jews remember that Esther stood up for what was right. She also trusted in God to help her win in the end.

Can you remember?

1 Jews build a little hut called a sukkah at _____.

2 The ceiling is hung with fruit because it is a _____ festival.

3 People wear fancy dress to _____ at Purim.

4 Jews remember the bravery of _____ in the readings at Purim.

Do you know?

What do the little huts at Sukkot remind Jews of?

6.6 Simchat Torah

The word simchat means to be happy. This is a festival when Jews are **happy** that God gave them the Torah. The festival is only celebrated in the synagogue. Jews do not celebrate this at home.

Let's begin again!

Jews read a piece of the Torah every week in the synagogue. By the end of the year the Jews will have read all of it. Simchat Torah is the day when they get to the end of the Torah. But as soon as they reach the end, they start again. This is to show the Torah goes on forever.

Dancing

The **services** at the synagogue on Simchat Torah are lively. Everybody wants to show how pleased they are. All the **scrolls** are taken out of the ark. The men who carry the scrolls dance around the synagogue with them seven times! People clap and sing as the scrolls go round. Children love it because they are given flags to wave and **sweets** to eat.

שמחת תורה

REJOICING OF THE LAW

- What do you think is in the middle of this flag? Pages 44–45 will help you.
- You can see the same type of picture on pages 14 and 16.

The dressed scrolls are brought out of the ark and carried around the synagogue.

Can you remember?

1 At Simchat Torah Jews are _____ that God gave the Torah to them.

2 There are lively _____ at the synagogue.

3 All the _____ are brought out of the ark.

4 Children enjoy it because they are given _____ and flags.

Do you know?

What do the men who carry the scrolls do?

6.7 Extension tasks

1

Draw a design for a Seder plate to be used at Passover. It can be any shape you like. In the middle you need to put a place for each of the special foods. You can copy the word Passover on it in Hebrew if you want to.

פֶּסַח

3

Look up Psalm 113. Copy out the first verse. Decorate the margin with harvest symbols for Sukkot.

2 Copy out the three sentences below that are true.

a) There are nine candles on the menorah at Hanukkah.
b) Purim is a very serious festival at the synagogue.
c) Jews fast at Yom Kippur.
d) Jews live outside in little huts at Sukkot.
e) Passover gets its name because Jews have to pass the bread over the table.

4 Act out this role play: a television interviewer asks a Jewish housewife about her spring-cleaning.

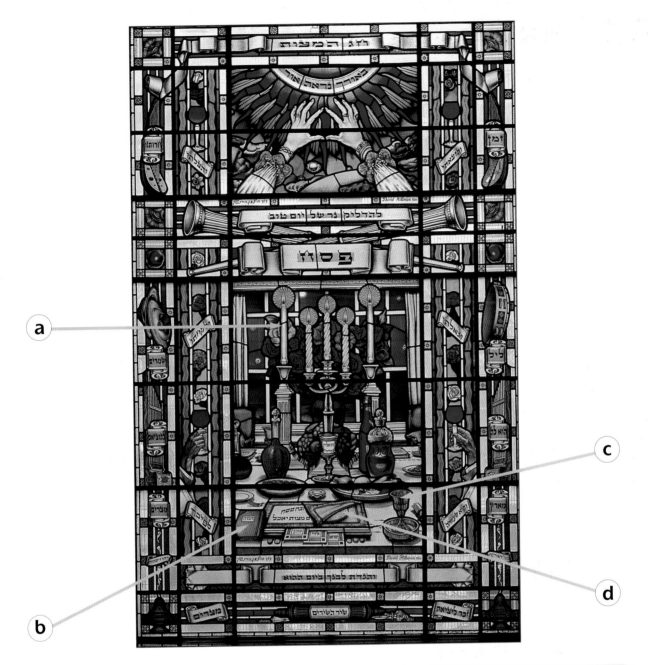

5 This synagogue window shows a Jewish festival.

a) Which festival is it?
b) How do you know?
c) Name each thing the arrows point to.
d) Why do you think the hands reach upwards?
e) Make a greetings card for this festival.

6

In groups of three or four make a poster called **JEWISH FESTIVALS**. Everybody in the group can choose a different festival. The poster must show:
• some of the festival story.
• some part of the modern festival.

Actress **Felicity Kendal** decided to become Jewish.
She used to be a Christian but she felt alone.

'I felt the need for some kind of **spiritual** base', she says. 'I am so happy I converted... I believe in the way that life and death are treated with an upfront acceptance and honesty. I like a set of rules whereby people know how to **behave** here and now, and not for the hereafter.'

Entertainer **Uri Geller** says:

'In early Jewish culture and religion, people were very superstitious. But why is Jewish magic so powerful, and why are so many magicians – including Houdini and David Copperfield – **Jewish**? Maybe it boils down to the God-given powers granted to Moses and the tribes of Israel thousands of years ago.'

Esther Rantzen started Childline. She says Jewish **family** life is important to her.

'Although we are a large family, we are a close one and all get on… even friends can blow hot and cold, but our feelings are that we are a united family and are always there for each other.'

Can you remember?

1 Uri Geller says many magicians are _____.

2 Felicity Kendal likes Judaism because it gives her a _____ base.

3 She also likes the rules about how to _____ in this life.

4 Esther Rantzen says Jewish _____ life is important to her.

Do you know?

Who does Uri Geller think God gave magic powers to in the past?

Steven Spielberg

Steven Spielberg is famous for making films like *ET* and *Jurassic Park*. He is also Jewish. He remembers how as a child some kids were cruel to him. 'I was always aware I stood out because of being Jewish. In high school I got smacked and kicked around. Two bloody noses. It was horrible.'

Schindler's List

Spielberg was delighted when he was asked to make the film *Schindler's List*. 'I've been preparing for this film my whole life', he said. He had heard stories of how his family had died in the **Holocaust**.

Oscar Schindler was a German factory owner and a Nazi. He used 1,100 Jews as unpaid workers. This stopped them being sent to the gas chambers.

An end to hatred

'It is a human story. And its subject matter applies to every nation',

Spielberg says. '*Schindler's List* is simply about racial hatred.' He hopes the film will make people aware that **racism** is evil. He also hopes it will put a stop to it.

Making the film was just the start for Spielberg. People came up to him when he was filming in eastern Europe. They were Holocaust **survivors** and wanted to tell him what had really happened. He began to record their stories on film as well.

'The most meaningful thing I have ever done', says Spielberg

This was the start of Survivors of the Shoah Visual History Foundation. This group is recording people's stories as quickly as possible because the people are elderly. There are stories about people who helped Jews to escape as well as survivors from the death camps.

Many interviews have been recorded already. It would take you over 13 years to watch them all! By 2004 Spielberg hopes to have 150,000 people's stories on the **Internet**.

Can you remember?

1 Steven Spielberg says _____ is evil.

2 He wanted to make *Schindler's List* because some of his family had died in the _____.

3 When he was making the film real _____ came up to talk to him.

4 Their stories are being put on the _____.

Do you know?

How far has Spielberg got with his website? Look it up on http://www.vhf.org

7.3 Concern for others

In the Torah it says God **created** the earth and all life on it. Jews think that the planet and its life should be treated with respect. They are told many times in the Torah how to do this.

God made **humans** above animals. An animal's life is never equal to a person's. Jews can eat meat if they want to, but the animal must be treated well and killed as quickly and as painlessly as possible.

Concern for animals

The Torah states that animals must be respected. In the Ten Commandments it says an animal must also rest on Shabbat like a human. But the Torah is clear that

Care of the environment

Jews believe they can use the world God created but they must not **destroy** it. This means they can cut down trees but must plant more.

Trees that are cut down must be replaced.

Care of others

The Torah says humans were made like God. Jews think this means it is very important to look after people. One way to do this is to give to charity to help poor people. They believe everyone can help someone poorer than themselves. Even those with no money can do **kind** deeds.

Some Jews give a tenth of their income to charity. Others give money at festival times, so poor people can have a good time too. To stop poor people feeling embarrassed about receiving help, there are Jewish charities. Poor people can be given help without everybody knowing about it. Nobody knows how much money a person gives to charity.

Can you remember?

1 Jews think they should look after the planet because God _____ it.

2 The Torah says that the lives of _____ are more important than animals.

3 Jews think they can use the planet but they must not _____ it.

4 Even poor people can help others by doing _____ actions.

Do you know?

Are Jews allowed to eat meat?

7.4 Never again!

Jews think it is important to remember things from the past. Good can come out of things even if they were bad. But it is hard to see what good came from the Holocaust.

Why remember the Holocaust?

The Chief Rabbi says: 'We don't remember for the sake of the past but for the sake of the future.' He says if we see people being treated badly today, we will want to help. By remembering the past, it will stop such evil happening again.

How do Jews remember the Holocaust?

Yad Vashem

The six million Jews killed by the Nazis have no **grave**. A park called Yad Vashem was created in Israel to remember them. It has a Hall of Remembrance in the middle where a **flame** burns all the time. Some ashes from each death camp are buried in front of the flame. Outside, **trees** are planted to remember people who were not Jews but who risked their life to help them. There is a memorial in the grounds to the one and a half million babies and children murdered by the Nazis.

This menorah shape is the logo of Yad Vashem. Each of the six candles stands for one million Jews killed by the Nazis.

Holocaust Day

Once a year Jews have a day to remember the victims. It is a quiet day when some people light **candles** and say prayers.

Outside Israel

People in other parts of the world remember the Holocaust because they never want it to happen again. There are groups in Britain and America.

This is the design planned for the new National Holocaust Museum to be built in Manchester. It represents shattered fragments.

Can you remember?

1 Yad Vashem was built because many Holocaust victims have no _____ .

2 There is a _____ that never goes out in the centre of the park.

3 _____ were planted to honour people who helped to save Jewish lives.

4 Some Jews light _____ to remember the dead on Holocaust Day.

Do you know?

Why do people want to remember the Holocaust?

7.5 Extension tasks

3 Can you research anything about Oscar Schindler? The facts may be different to the film version.

4 In groups of two or three make a poster to show how Jews care for the world. You may focus on one aspect if you wish.

1 Holocaust Day is the anniversary of the Warsaw ghetto uprising. It was a time in the Second World War when Jews tried to defeat the Nazis. Can you discover any more details about it?

2 Write 100 words to go in a tourist guide. Tell the tourists what Yad Vashem is. Why should people go there?

5 These beauty products above are made from Dead Sea mud and sold all over the world. What can you find out about the Dead Sea that makes it so special?

6 Read this article from a newspaper.

- You can access Benjamin Cohen's website on www.Jewishnet.co.uk
- Why would Jews find it helpful?
- Design a new opening page for this website.

Jewish website nets London schoolboy £5m

■ A schoolboy aged 17 has had his Internet website valued at up to £5 million, after being in business for only seven months.

■ Since Benjamin Cohen, who attends the Jewish Free School in London, started Jewishnet.co.uk, the site has had 2.2 million visitors. It has also attracted the attention of big business and Benjamin is set to join the list of successful British Internet entrepreneurs.

■ His idea was simple: to put the large Jewish community in Britain in touch with Jewish businesses. His website is the equivalent of a Jewish Yellow Pages, enabling people to find everyone from a Jewish candlestick maker to a Jewish plumber.

'I wanted to do something good for the community,' Benjamin said. 'But it was also a market that hadn't been tapped into – there are not a lot of people tapping into the Jewish brand.'

■ The brand idea appeals to Benjamin, who sees Judaism not only as a religion but also as a way of life. 'It has', he says ' "brand loyalty". If [Jewish] people see Freeserve or Screaming Net, then see a Jewish alternative, they will go with that.' As well as business, the site deals with the community's spiritual and emotional needs: Alan Plancey, its online 'Cyber Rabbi', receives more than a thousand religious queries a month.

© Ben Hammersley, The Times, London, 2 September 1999

Glossary

A

Abraham the founder of Judaism.
Ark the cupboard where the scrolls are kept.

B

Bar Mitzvah the ceremony when a 13-year-old boy begins religious duties.
Bat Mitzvah the ceremony when a 12-year-old girl begins religious duties.
Bedouin people who live a wandering life in tents in Israel.
Bet Din the court of three or more rabbis who decide on Jewish laws like food.
Breastplate a silver decoration hanging on a scroll.
Brit Milah the circumcision of an eight-day-old Jewish baby boy.

C

Canaan an old name for Israel.
Cantor the person who leads the prayers by chanting in a synagogue.
Circumcise to remove the foreskin of the penis.
Covenant the promise made between God and the Jews.

D

Dead Sea scrolls old pieces of scriptures found in a cave in 1947.
Dressed scrolls scrolls with a covering and decorations.

E

Elijah a major Jewish prophet.

H

Hanukkah a winter festival of lights.
Havdalah a ceremony at the end of Shabbat.
Hebrew the language of the Jewish religion.
Holocaust the name for the Nazi murder of the Jews.
Huppah the wedding canopy.

I

Israel the Jewish homeland set up in 1948.

J

Jerusalem the holy city for Jews set up by King David.

K

Ketubah a Jewish marriage contract.

Kippah a skullcap worn by Jewish males.

Kittel a white robe worn by men at Yom Kippur.

Kosher means right or correct and is usually used to describe food.

L

Lulav a bunch of palm, willow and myrtle branches waved at the festival of Sukkot.

M

Mantle the cover of a scroll.

Matzos crackers made without yeast and eaten specially at Passover.

Mazel Tov 'Good luck!' in Hebrew.

Menorah a seven-branched candlestick.

Mezuzah the scroll in a box nailed to a door frame.

Mount Sinai the mountain where Moses received the Torah from God.

P

Palestine the name that used to be used for Israel.

Passover the main Jewish festival in the Spring.

Pharaoh an Egyptian king.

Promised Land the country Jews believe God gave them.

Psalms songs written by King David.

Purim a festival that celebrates trust in God.

Q

Quill a feather pen used to write the scrolls.

R

Rabbi a Jewish religious teacher.

Rosh Hashanah the Jewish New Year festival.

S

Scribe the person who writes the scrolls by hand.

Scrolls rolls of parchment containing passages of scripture.

Seder plate a special dish with foods used at Passover.

Shabbat Jewish holy day.

Shalom 'peace' in Hebrew.

Shema the most important Jewish prayer.

Shoah the Hebrew name for the Holocaust.

Shofar the ram's horn blown at Jewish New Year.

Simchat Torah the festival to thank God for the scriptures.

Spice box a scented box used at the end of Shabbat.

Star of David the six pointed star that is a symbol of Judaism.

Sukkah little huts used during the festival of Sukkot.

Sukkot the harvest festival.

Synagogue the Jewish place of worship.

T

Tallit a shawl worn for morning prayer.

Tefillin small boxes containing prayers worn by men on the head and arm.

Temple the holy building in Jerusalem destroyed in 70 CE.

Ten Commandments the rules God gave to Moses on two pieces of stone.

Ten Plagues the ten disasters God brought on the Egyptians.

Torah the five books of scripture God gave to Moses, containing the laws.

W

Western Wall the last piece of the Temple in Jerusalem. It is a holy place.

Y

Yad a pointer used to read the scrolls.

Yad Vashem a memorial park in Jerusalem dedicated to Holocaust victims.

Yahrzeit candle a memorial candle lit on the anniversary of a death.

Yom Kippur the last day of the Jewish New Year when people fast. A holy day.

Glossary